CHANGE VELOCITY

The Secret to Leading a Successful Sales Transformation

Charlie Thackston

authorHOUSE®

AuthorHouse™
1663 Liberty Drive
Bloomington, IN 47403
www.authorhouse.com
Phone: 1 (800) 839-8640

Published by AuthorHouse 10/06/2016

ISBN: 978-1-5246-4182-5 (sc)
ISBN: 978-1-5246-4181-8 (hc)
ISBN: 978-1-5246-4183-2 (e)

Library of Congress Control Number: 2016915933

Print information available on the last page.

This book is printed on acid-free paper.

ACKNOWLEDGMENTS

I want to thank my colleagues at SOAR Performance Group for their collaboration and contributions to this book. I want to thank my present and past clients for the opportunity to experience and support their transformations. I want to thank my mother, Evelyn, for giving me a passion for writing. I want to thank my Dad, C.A., for instilling a work ethic that has served me well. I want to thank my daughter, Grace, for her support in editing this book. I want to thank my son, John, for inspiring me to accomplish more than originally planned with this book. Most of all, I would like to thank my wife, Gayle, for supporting me through all of the business adventures and providing a thoughtful perspective when needed. And, not to miss the opportunity to say thank you for all of my many blessings. Life is good!

My final thank you is to you. Thank you for honoring me with the opportunity to share perspectives, experiences, insights, and opinions that I sincerely hope will make a difference for you in leading transformation in your organization. The words that follow are from the school where my Dad learned much, the school of hard knocks. Experience is a wonderful teacher. I wish you success in leading change that will transform your organization.

CONTENTS

INTRODUCTION

In today's world of breakneck change, many business transformations fail. It's not because the ideas fueling the change aren't necessary or good ideas, but because they do not happen fast enough. This is very apparent when you look at the rapid rate of changes in leadership from CEO to President to Vice President of Sales to Chief Information Officer, to name a few. Just take a look in your financial journals, newsfeeds, and business blogs; it is common to see rapid changes in the executive ranks. With tenures of less than two years for key leadership roles such as the Vice President of Sales, how can a CEO drive the changes required for transformation in go-to-market strategy or customer experience? Short tenure in role is simply a lagging indicator of the problem, so what is the cause of these types of short tenure statistics? In this book, we will explore why the rate of change is accelerating in the market, why transformation is required, and how to make it happen.

Over the past 16 years, I have helped companies deal with rapidly changing business environments. Previously, I invested a dozen years growing two companies from early phase start-up to successful initial public offerings in sales leadership, marketing, field operations and product development roles. My real passion is helping businesses grow. This frequently requires transformation within the organization. What is **transformation**? A change in form, appearance, nature or character. As I looked at this sequence of words defining transformation, I started to think that changes in all these areas—in form, appearance, nature *and* character—are required for a business transformation. Transformation is a tall order. However, the really tall order is the ability to deliver transformation at the speed required in the rapidly accelerating pace of change today.

This book will focus on the need for **Change Velocity**, what I believe to be the secret to leading successful business transformations. While reading the book, keep the following formula in mind.

Change Velocity = Change View x Change Reaction x Change Motivation

Why do I believe that Change Velocity is the key to organizational transformation? Because, people are at the heart of every transformation. People determine the change view, change reaction, and change motivation that create the ability to change at the speed necessary today. To lead in today's world is to initiate change. We must deploy new go-to market strategies, new supporting processes, new supporting tools, and new management approaches. Our ability to lead and create Change Velocity in our organizations is imperative for organizational health. I hope this book will enable you to make the changes you need to make in your organization. Each chapter is filled with keywords, bold and underlined, which you can find in the back in Appendix A. Each chapter also ends with key questions to help you determine your steps forward. These can be found in Appendix B and form the basis for your transformation checklist to understand the actions required to lead your own transformation. Now, let's learn about Change Velocity!

CHAPTER ONE:

WHY DOES CHANGE HAPPEN FAST?

Change happens fast in today's world. The increasingly rapid pace of change is happening due to **3 Pivot Factors:** Rapid Dissemination, Faster Creation, and Time To. While Rapid Dissemination and Faster Creation have fairly obvious meanings, you may wonder at the meaning of Time To. Time To is all about speed of achieving an expected outcome. This speed to expected outcome is accelerating with the rate of change in the business world today.

RAPID DISSEMINATION

Rapid dissemination happens in every sector now because of greater connectivity and greater proximity of that connectivity.

Information, knowledge, experiences, opinions and perspectives are instantly available as we glance ever so frequently at our mobile devices. I believe mobile devices will all soon be **Wearables**. Who could have imagined twenty years ago that we would be able to wear phones or computers? My forecast for 2030 is that Wearables will become **Thinkables**, devices that respond to our thoughts rather than our physical or verbal commands. This is the effect of Rapid Dissemination, as it continues to spark new thoughts, we imagine more. Beyond my forecast of Thinkables for 2030, my forecast for 2050 will be the migration from Wearables to Thinkables to **Imaginables** as the ability to imagine will be translated through Thinkable designs to 3D Printers that generate one-of-a-kind products unimaginable to us in our current frame of possibilities today.

The breadth and depth of information is continuously expanding through the connection to everything from our televisions, to our thermostats, to our appliances and many more applications in the commercial world. All of this connectedness, now referred to as the Internet of Things, is accelerating the dissemination of information. In 2006, we worked on a strategic initiative with a global communications company to support the launch of their Machine-to-Machine, now known as Internet of Things, business development initiative. At the time, they had to look for applications for Machine-to-Machine communications to seed the space with real business applications. How the world has changed! Now, we must simply take a look around our office, our home, our car, or even our bathroom to see an opportunity for connectivity in this world of the Internet of Things.

Why this change from looking for applications for connectivity to responding to opportunities for connectivity? The answer lies in the ability to connect, collect information, and make the information *actionable*. We supported an initiative for one of our clients to drive the selling of Innovation to their clients. Many of the success stories that participants shared as a part of the initiative were due to the power of Rapid Dissemination resulting in action. There were stories regarding using geospatial location information to protect and conserve trees in rapidly developing cities. There were stories of delivering point of location information to guide visitors in exploring all there is to offer in an exciting city such as Barcelona. There were stories of optimizing the flow of use and servicing for the bathroom facilities at major sporting events. We can all relate to the experience of missing that most important play during a sporting event as we dashed off to the facilities to find a long line. Rapid collection and dissemination of information from the point of interaction creates the opportunity to drive better outcomes and, most importantly, the opportunity for each of us not to miss that big play, whether on the sporting field or the business field. These are all examples of the change resulting from the Rapid Dissemination of information driven by greater connectivity, greater bandwidth, and greater capacity to use the information.

Connectivity, Bandwidth and Capacity are the technology capabilities enabling Rapid Dissemination. However, capability at the corporate level does not indicate desire from the customer or user perspective. What is happening at the customer level that is creating the desire for Rapid Dissemination? In my view, it all started with the introduction of *self-serve* pay at the local gas pump. I refer to it as the **Gas Pump Phenomenon**. I was happy in my youth to pull into a service station, wait for an attendant to come to my car, ask him to "fill 'er up" and then view through the mirrors and windshield as they filled the tank, checked the oil, checked the other fluids, soaped and squeegeed the windows clean. It was probably a ten-minute process, and you frequently met a very engaging attendant. This was in the day when gasoline cost 35 cents per gallon. Today, I pay five to ten times as much for the gasoline, pump it myself and certainly do not get very much entertainment at the pumps. And I get to squeegee my windows, check my oil and check the fluids by myself, if it happens at all. So, what do we get from all of this self-service that started with the gas pump? We get freedom to do things when we want and as fast as we want. If the line looks long at one station, I just go to another, which is usually right across the street with prices that are fairly consistent. If I am in a hurry, rather than filling the entire tank, I just get enough fuel for now and "fill 'er up" later. Self-service creates a more direct connection to the customer as information is collected about the specific customer's buying interactions from transactional information to buying patterns to frequency of purchase to their shopping basket of purchases. Connectivity makes the capture of all of this information possible. More importantly, the collection creates the opportunity for Rapid Dissemination.

A side effect of Rapid Dissemination is a changing information relationship between the businesses selling the products to the end customer, the distributors and the manufacturers. A new transparency becomes possible for the understanding of who the customer is and what they are buying. This transparency creates new expectations in the relationship and sometimes eliminates the need for intermediaries in transactions within the supply chain. New, simpler business networks are formed or new, simpler networks displace the existing network. Let's consider the retailing effect of what is referred to as show rooming. The shopper sees a product in the retailer's show room or store; immediately starts to check features and capabilities for comparable or same products on their smart phone. They no longer have to go from physical store to physical store to compare prices or even make a phone call. Much of the information is instantly available at the potential customer's fingertips.

Just think of all the immediate access to information that we have as the result of our Smart Phones. Have you ever enjoyed sitting around and bantering back and forth about sports, history, movies, or music? Who was the 1982 NCAA college football champion? Who won the 1996 baseball World Series? Who was the news reporter that cracked the Watergate scandal? Which rock and roll band had the number one hit of 1978? Who won the OSCAR for best Actor in 2008? Where is Bali? When these types of questions come up today, watch the fingers start moving as everyone types the questions into their Smart Phone as quickly as possible. It is no longer about whether you know the information, but how quickly can you access it. All this is the power of Rapid Dissemination, access to information and the ability to use information.

FASTER CREATION

Faster Creation of products, services and expertise is the reality of today and will be the reality of tomorrow. Speed is critical to success with customers and markets. It is all the result of the Gas Pump Phenomenon. We now have self-serve gas, food, customer service, technical help and even love. Find the love of your life, all through your "self-serve dating site". I found mine the old fashioned way: I walked her home from a party and even talked as we walked, rather than texting. This is a novel idea in today's world of virtual connections. Connections between people are created faster, as well as products. Take car production, for instance. New car models are now introduced much quicker than they were in the past. This is all the result of computer-aided design and new platform-based production processes. This results in efficiency through common core designs for frames and foundational components across models, creating economies of scale in sourcing, production equipment and production processes. We have all of this efficiency paired with the ability to tailor the design of your own personal car, taking the concept of self-service and personalization to a whole new level. As I mentioned earlier, I believe we will soon move into the era of Imaginables, where the consumer is able to think of and create their own product. I am fascinated by the 3D printing industry and the possibilities as we move from self-service to self-creation.

This is not so different from the early pioneers in America who, upon realizing a need, designed it and made it—from tools for tending the fields to log cabins for shelter. As the world moved to division of labor for productivity and scale, this one-man connection between thought, design and creation was separated into more distinct functions. This now frequently involves silo organizations, causing some of the drag on the speed of change within many commercial organizations. So, maybe those in our day and age are the new pioneers with the opportunity to create a vast array and large quantity of objects with less labor and time. Faster Creation in terms of products, services and expertise means new business models are created and new industries spawned. Virtual communities create the opportunity for new interconnected networks of businesses and people for driving new business opportunities. New communities share expertise that helps the community advance quickly in solving complex needs. It creates a self-service learning environment where learning is delivered through virtual on the job training brought to you instantly by the experiences of others. Faster Creation of knowledge and skills is driving faster results. Faster Creation seems to be focused on even faster production of personalized products. But does Faster Creation beget simplicity? Is the seeming convenience of self-service or self-creation really convenient?

The possibilities and potential for Faster Creation will bring new opportunities for personalized products, services and expertise. Additionally, individualized creation will reduce the need for collaboration in the design and development process. On the expertise front, I have experienced Faster Creation in my research efforts to learn more about the history of my family. Using an online genealogy research site, I was able to generate multiple branches of my family with detail facts on locations, dates and events with personalized hints served up on a continuing basis as I added more information. The tool learned about my family, then served up the relevant genealogical information to help me rapidly build my family tree. Faster Creation in this case took much of the expertise required for genealogical research and delivered it directly to me. This created an altogether different and better customer experience.

TIME TO

So, what is **Time To** all about? There is a short Time To expectation for everything. Let's name a few of the Time To's:

1. Time To - Customer Delight
2. Time To - Benefit
3. Time To - Value
4. Time To - Return on Investment
5. Time To - Launch of a New Product
6. Time To - Win a New Customer
7. Time To - Deploy a Solution
8. Time To - Get a Question Answered
9. Time To - Receive Your Product or Service

You get it. The Time To expectations have changed. This is one of the key reasons for the increase in the rate of change. When the customer expectations for Time To change, so do the demands for acceleration and demands for time contraction. I grew up in the construction business, and my Dad frequently said, "Time is money". That certainly is true today. You are either making money or spending money, depending on where your organization is in your impact on the Time To pivot factor. Your focus has to shift to the "How To"- how to respond and anticipate the "Time To" requirements of your customers. How to reduce time to benefit, time to value, time to return on investment, time to customer delight, and any additional time expectations of your customers.

So, the question for each business and organization is what Time To levers affect your organization? If you do not focus on them, a new or existing competitor will. Time To can be a disruptive factor in many industries. Take a look at the disruptive nature of digital commerce where we simply search, point, click and buy, all in the comfort of our own homes. No longer are we required to drive or walk to a store to search for what we want, then go to another store for comparison of options and prices. One example of a business identifying and meeting Time To needs comes from a very busy Starbucks location near our office in Atlanta. The location is filled with busy executives, families and students hurrying in for their coffee order in this walk-in only location. The result between 6:30 am and 9:00 am is a very crowded store with a usual line of 8 to 10 people. Voila, a solution addressing time to customer delight and time to benefit rescues the day with online ordering. You simply walk in and pick up your coffee ready to go, as the transaction is complete before you arrive. So, adding to our list of Time To's is the Time To - Coffee reducing the Time To - Perk Up for the day.

As a part of our work with clients, we have traditionally asked them to identify the internal and external influences that are causing their business to change. When it comes to the accelerating pace of change today, it is important not only to think about the influences driving change, but also to understand how Rapid Dissemination, Faster Creation and Time To are impacting your customers and your industry. What new business networks, ecosystems or communities (your customers, the suppliers to your customer, your customers' customers) are being formed as a result of these pivot factors in your industry and your customers' industries. These new business networks are reshaping industries as distribution layers are removed and connections become more direct through online interactions that shift the relationship from multi-layer engagement channels to direct exchange.

After 17 years in the technology industry growing young venture capital backed software companies, I began consulting. As a consultant, I have experienced and helped drive many a transformation as the markets and businesses have changed. As an executive leader in developing private companies to be public companies, this required an even more substantial transformation. Both good and bad transformation happens as you move from a start-up to a public company. A start-up is agile, constantly looking for the sweet spot for growth in the market, while a public company has requirements for predictable and repeatable results to satisfy the investment community. These two types of companies have very different needs. In my transition from software industry executive to consultant, I learned quickly that the best way to start a consulting engagement was with a diagnostic of the client's needs. Rarely was there an argument from the clients about the need for a diagnostic when we engaged with them in the early 2000's. The clients were generally very receptive to the approach of doing a diagnostic including a series of interviews with leadership, top performers and thought leaders within the organization to understand what was working, what was not working and what the top performers did differently from the rest of the team. More importantly, we strove to determine how we could create a repeatable process that leveraged what the top performers were doing in their typical unconscious competent state. You have probably seen someone who is extremely successful on a repeatable basis, yet unaware of how they do it when asked. We got very good at discerning secrets to their success through structured interviews and assessments we could use to build the secret sauce for the rest of the organization. The Client leadership always found the results of the diagnostic interviews very useful, with high impact actionable recommendations to move the needle in the business.

This unconscious competent situation reminds me of my summer days as a young boy. On an early Saturday morning when we were not working, I enjoyed going fishing at any one of the small lakes within a bike's ride of where I lived in a then small town of Marietta, Georgia. One of the fishing lakes of my youth near my parent's former home is still there. The others have gone the way of development; where the fish lived, there are now homes and apartments. As a boy, I would arrive at the lake with my fishing pole, fishing tackle box, water and a snack in case the fishing continued past the ever-important lunchtime. Upon arrival at the lake, there would usually be few older men fishing ahead of me. I guess they did not take time for Saturday morning cartoons before fishing. Soon, I would start my rounds to check out what had happened before I arrived, hoping someone was not in my favorite spot under the willow trees. After a few years of fishing the lakes in the area, I was familiar with the types of fish in each of the lakes, which bait historically worked best, which times of day to held the greatest likelihood of catching a large fish. Regardless of this experience, I always asked the same questions when I arrived. "Did you catch anything?" "What kind of fish was it?" "How big was it?" "What bait are they biting?" "How was the fight landing the fish?" The last one to slip in just after the tale of the fight to get the fish ashore was: "Where did you catch it?" Through these questions and experiences fishing the lakes near our home, I became quite a good small lake fisherman for a young boy. I was your unconscious competent, catching trophy fish and not knowing they were trophy fish, not quite able to explain to others how I had done it. I knew the lakes. I knew what types of fish were in each lake. I knew the baits that worked best for the fish in each lake. I knew the best spots from my own experience and the answers to the questions I asked of the older men fishing the lakes.

When I think back, I believe the real skill beyond the knowledge of the lakes, the knowledge of the fish, the bait and the time of day, was the gift of patience, which is not the gift of most young boys. To me, the lakes were more magical than even the lunchtime I frequently forgot as I emptied my thoughts, gazing into the lakes looking after the big one. I was patient, but never passive or complacent! I worked the best spots, tried different baits, used different movements of the lures through the water, kept a feel for the tension in the fishing line and kept a positive perspective. Maybe this is the reason I have enjoyed the field of sales and sales performance. I refer to myself as a proactively patient person, patient and confident that the big fish are there, but proactively driving the changes required in catching them. Fishing conditions change quickly in a day with variations in temperature, the amount of the light, and the locations of insects on the lake. Sounds like the business environment of today. Maybe fishing was the training ground for understanding the need to change in response to changing conditions influencing my opportunity to land the big fish.

ACCELERATING TIME TO

Now, based on my fishing experiences as a boy, I learned the real value of a good set of diagnostic questions and their impact on performance. But the world of sales performance consulting is the world of Time To. The question from the clients always was and is: "Can you do it faster?" The clients have lived with inefficiencies and problems for years, in many cases finding a way to muscle through them. When we are engaged, even if the decision process took 6-12 months, they have endured and want the benefits of the new approach now, not tomorrow. The 2009 start of the Great Recession only increased the pressure, elongating the decision process, limiting funds available, and amplifying Time To requirements. For us as a business, the increasing demands for Time To were right up our ally, as we constantly focused on acceleration of our work to create value faster and with greater impact for our clients. Independent reviews of initiatives that we had driven resulted in hundreds of millions in incremental revenue and margin for our select set of clients. We addressed this demand for faster time to diagnostic results with a simple online survey approach. We lost the ability to build buy-in through the diagnostic participants, which is extremely powerful in driving a transformational initiative.

So, we decided to develop the SOAR Interactive Survey Session, which integrated interactive surveys at large team events, such as national sales meetings, with team discussion and work group outputs during the sessions. The result accelerated diagnostic time, provided greater buy-in, allowed the capture of example situations, and generated a faster Time To for the client. We recently used this Interactive Survey Session with a mid-market software company at a meeting of around 250 participants. In four hours, we engaged the group, captured perspectives relative to customer and account management success guides, plus generated the front-line perspectives that we coveted so much for our later work. The North American leader for the group said it was exactly what the team needed as they readied for the transformation ahead from territory management to key account management. What would have taken months five years ago was done in 4 hours, and the client saw acceleration in the launch of the overall initiative and greater buy-in from the teams.

I want to leave you with **three questions** to consider as you look ahead for your next transformational pivot factors:

1. How is "Rapid Dissemination" impacting your customers, their customers and their suppliers?
2. How is "Faster Creation" impacting your customers, their customers and their suppliers?
3. How is "Time To" impacting your customers, their customers and their suppliers?

Bottom line question for you: Is your organization ready to deal with the accelerating rate of change?

CHAPTER TWO:

WHAT IS CHANGE VELOCITY?

When defining **velocity**, I prefer the mechanics definition, which is the time rate of change of position of a body in a specified direction.

THE MECHANICS OF TRANSFORMATION

I did not receive the same mechanic gene that my father and my brother received. The closest I have come to being a mechanic is in fixing problems in businesses. As a boy, I did not enjoy repairing the paving equipment belonging to my dad's company. I looked forward to a day when I would no longer have to be covered in the grease involved in those repairs. As a man, I have escaped the grease, but not the mess involved in mechanics. Driving change initiatives for our clients requires some of those same mechanic skills of diagnosing the situation, understanding how to get things running, and then delivering value for the clients.

After my father passed away in 2002, I had to jump back into his business after being away for 22 years. The knowledge I had developed while working with him in my youth and the skills I had developed in the business world came in handy as we had to kick-start his small business following his death. My dad had been the heart, soul, and momentum of that company. I quickly assessed the situation, spoke to the small remaining crew and realized that they needed and wanted to work. I felt a responsibility to help them work, if they wanted to work. So, I set about estimating, quoting, and selling the work at lunch, in the evening, over the weekend, or by phone when travelling, as I was still fully engaged in my consulting business. I quickly had a backlog of work and some very large projects queued up for the crew. I had thought that once I kick-started the business with a few projects, they would be on their way. One of the very first projects was a large parking lot that I was proud to have sold. When I took the crew over to view the project and discuss the timelines, they started to name off all the equipment needed that was in disrepair. For those with experience around equipment, when it is no longer useful, you can sell it for the value it has at that time, or you can store it for use of the parts in an area affectionately called the "bone yard".

Reminiscent of the situations many entrepreneurial leaders have experienced in out-selling operational capacity, I briefly fretted over what I had signed the crew up for, then quickly assessed the situation. We decided what needed repair and how quickly we could get the repairs done. We repaired a dump truck that my Father and I had purchased together some 18 years prior. Incredibly, we had it cranked and running in a few days without a very substantial amount of money or time investment. The motor graders were a different story. A motor grader is used for leveling the ground and spreading the gravel base in a parking lot installation.

Motor Grader

The larger of the two in disrepair was an ancient Caterpillar Grader from the 60's that I had seen complete many a large job, but the mid size Puckett was much more nimble for smaller jobs. We decided that we needed both ready for this project. The CAT was up and running after just a few days. The only issue was that the experienced operator for this equipment had moved on years ago. Now the Puckett grader was in much worse condition than I had realized. It was a real investment in time and money to get it up and running, due to the specialized parts and extensive labor required for the repair. It's exhilarating, for those who have worked in the grease to make the transformation happen, when a piece of equipment comes back to life after sitting idle in a bone yard for many years. Suddenly, there is a deep roar as the engine starts up and the equipment is moving as if simply awakening from a deep sleep. You may never experience equipment coming back to life, but the same is true for an old house or an old piece of furniture finding new life. The roar is not quite the same, but the joy of transformation certainly is. For me, the thrill is the same when a business, a sales team, or an individual team member finds new life.

Let's remember our definition of Change Velocity: "the time to change the direction of an organization or individual to align with a desired transformation". How long does it take for an organization or an individual to change direction in order to align with the new transformational strategy? The movement of direction is key in this assessment. If the sales force has been calling on Small Medium Business accounts and you now want them to call on Large Enterprise Accounts, how long will it take to get the change in direction of activity? If service managers have traditionally focused on problem resolution, but you want them to focus on relationships with key customers to support expansion in services, how long will it take to change the direction of focus and activity? If your key managers spend the majority of their time focused on operations and minimal time on strategy and people, how long will it take to make this shift in focus? Change Velocity measures the time it takes to shift the direction of activity, as well as the time it takes to get from where you are today to where you want to be in the future. The real joy in transformation lies in seeing individuals, organizations and businesses have a better opportunity, as we have seen in our clients through many of our programs.

ANTICIPATING THE TURNING POINT

How does all of this relate to Change Velocity, "the time to change the direction of an organization or individual to align with a desired transformation"? The time for changing direction and moving in a new direction matters! It matters because, as mentioned in the introduction, most transformations fail, even those founded in necessary ideas. You see it in the rapid turnover in leadership positions in organizations as they look for the pivot factors that will allow them to deal with Rapid Dissemination, Faster Creation and Time To. How will they make the turn in direction quickly enough to make it happen? Now, I am not a racecar driver, but a friend who has a deep interest in fast cars shared that in racecar driving, there is a concept referred to as the **turning point**. My understanding is that the cars, approaching 120+ miles per hour, have a reaction dilemma due to their speed of movement. So, the drivers must look ahead to the turning point in order to react to the turn in advance of getting there. When this was explained to me, I understood the need to look ahead to the turning point and thought I would try this concept in safe manner at the legal speed limit while driving through some mountain roads. You know how mountain roads can be- with switchbacks curving up the mountain, interspersed with straight sections of road as you come over the crest of the mountain and start down. Typically, a curve lies ahead as you move through the straights. I found it somewhat difficult to focus on the curve ahead with large semi-trucks shifting around me. I remember times when the winds were so heavy that the semi-trucks looked as if they would be pushed off the road, and me with them.

This issue of anticipating change is exactly the same issue for leaders within an organization. They must be looking ahead to the turning point. However, there is the constant distraction of daily business operations, employee issues, large massive competitors and small nimble competitors, resulting in a focus on short-term reactions and priorities. There are the semi-trucks, or competitors, shifting into your lane. Then, the unexpected headwinds and crosswinds, the market forces creating pressure on the business through a drag resistance, slowing you down or pushing in an unexpected direction. There are the ever-changing road hazards, from ice to falling rocks. The art of leadership lies in staying on the road that leads to your destination while avoiding the hazards and overcoming the obstacles. The destination is the priority.

One of my colleagues captured this very thinking in our strategy development and messaging methodology that we refer to as Stratimation^SM - "Strategy Acceleration through Animation". We created this methodology in collaboration with a very talented creative firm. We found it incredibly rewarding as we took our strategic planning framework and in a matter of hours were able to create a strategic vision with the messaging to support communication across the organization. We experienced the power of creative thinking with strong proven methodology and powerful visual animation. After thinking about this experience with the Stratimation^SM methodology, it was clear that both the beauty and power are in the simplicity. One of our organization's strengths is the ability to take the complexity of our client's business and simplify the complexity to support effective execution. Two essential steps in simplifying are essential to creating Change Velocity as well. First, clarify what the strategy is. Second, clearly communicate the strategy in a compelling manner. As you may have experienced, this is much easier said than done.

Our work in this area of strategy development and messaging started a number of years ago when we supported a communications industry executive in driving execution of the strategy for a new business unit he was leading. In our own experiences in leadership roles with fast growing start-ups, we had developed and executed strategies for growth, new go-to-markets, new target customers, new vertical markets and new operational models to support execution of the strategies. However, we had never really codified the strategy development, strategy communication and strategy execution elements we were successfully using. As we started this process of considering what was required to focus on the turning point for this communication industry executive's business unit, I thought back to a comment one of my colleagues made: "the answers you get are in the questions you ask". This became the core thinking as we considered how to structure a meaningful and effective dialogue around strategy execution to drive Change Velocity.

While the perceived need was for more operational discipline within the sales organization, the aperture of the lens began to open more widely as we asked the simple question- "Where do you want to be?" There is much discussion in strategy sessions around where the organization is. Generally, this discussion around current situation is driven by the historical focus on financial reporting, which is all about reporting the results of what has happened. Understanding what has happened is important, as we can certainly learn from the past. The real goal, however, is to do the things that will effectively move us to where we want to be in the future. The business unit that this communications industry executive inherited was in a fading segment of the business resulting from a relatively small acquisition focused on the multi-tenant building segment (apartments, condominiums, new residential developments). As he assessed where he wanted to be, the very first focus was on the potential within the multi-tenant market and what the competitors in their market (the semi-trucks in their roadway) were doing. The potential was there, but where was the turning point that would create the opportunity to expand and grow in this segment of customers? The big question was "where do you want to be"? With this being a new business unit for this executive, there was a rapid ramp-up to quickly assess current situation as a foundation for movement to where they wanted to be. The opportunity started to be redefined as the capability to reach the potential customers was somewhat defined by accessible locations or future accessible locations for the technology. The need to strategically view capabilities available and future availability in line with the market potential became a key pivot point for the organization. The second pivot point lay in understanding the capabilities of the semi-trucks in their roadway. What lanes were competitors currently in? When and how would they change lanes? Which lane was the communications company in? When and how would they want to change lanes? Where was the turning point ahead? The road analogy became an easy way to bring the perspective that is required for strategic thinking. You can move quickly into an existing lane or make a turn (pivot) to a new road. Or when it comes to true innovation, create a new way to travel where the current roads are no longer important.

WHERE DO YOU WANT TO BE?

Out of this experience, our thinking for strategy development crystallized into three key questions:

- Where do we want to be?
- Where are we?
- How do we get there?

You may think it logical to start with where you are, then ask where you want to be. But the sequence of questions is tremendously important. The question of where we want to be often becomes a filler question for the end of a strategy discussion after reams of information and discussion on where we are. Starting with considering where you want to be creates a subtle but powerful change in flow forcing a forward view. Now for this to work, there is a requirement for preparation of the team to be ready with core understanding of the business' current situation. Otherwise, you end up with a current state diagnosis vs. a future-focused strategy discussion. This thinking is more difficult, but leads to an optimal balance of 80% focus on the future and 20% focus on the past in a strategy session. Just as in life, the past can hold us back. We can learn from the past, but we can't change it.

Change Velocity requires a clear focus on the future and what that future will look like. One of our clients in Europe says that you must clearly understand and focus on your ambition. What do you want the business or organization to be? When you focus intently on this question, it will support you later in a critical aspect of Change Velocity: prioritizing what is important. An organization must know its focus. A potential client recently told us they were executing twenty work streams to drive their strategy. To help them create real focus, we recommended they identify which 3 work streams would really move the needle for the business. That is where the session ended, leaving the group to contemplate what the real priorities were. Knowing your ambition for the business –where you want to be–is critical.

So, it was through our work at SOAR that we noticed the need for clients to focus on Change Velocity specific to their organization. We saw transformation after transformation announced and never accomplished, due to the inability to achieve the desired future state in a time relevant for the market situation. Recommendations from large strategy firms frequently sound the same in the business-to-business sales space. Segment your customers into enterprise, mid-market and mass market segments. Create a pyramid slide with slices. Then, establish specific resource allocation and coverage models focusing resources where there is the greatest opportunity. Making it actually happen is easier said than done. Executives find their desk littered with large binders, their email littered with large PowerPoint decks and PDF documents marked confidential and proprietary. Best practices around strategy development, targeting of customers and customer coverage models are certainly good if they are proven and work for your organization. Making it work is all about execution. Best practices in strategy development can be a great way to identify market focus and potential gains in operational efficiency as well as effectiveness. However, when everyone in your market has the same basic strategy packaged and delivered by the same firms, what will the real differentiation be? A differentiated strategy is about changing the game, doing it differently and creating a strategic advantage so customers understand your unique value compared to the competition.

Out of all of this discussion of 'what to do' is a crying need for a discussion of how to do it, which is where we have added value for our clients over the years. The 'how to' is where the rubber meets the road, a phrase frequently used by one of the executives at the first software company I worked at in the mid 1980's. Rubber meeting the road is required for Change Velocity. The rubber meets the road most frequently where your front line staff engages with customers, partners, suppliers and each other to make the change happen. People create traction or reduce traction for the change through their willingness and ability. The processes and tools deployed to create repeatability for the change are all deeply impacted by the willingness and ability of the people engaged in driving the change. Creating Change Velocity requires addressing the willingness (attitude) and the ability (knowledge & skills) in order to pivot to the new direction and accelerate from A to Z, from where you are now to where you want to be.

I want to leave you with three questions to consider as you strategically accelerate from where you are to where you want to be:

1. How clear is the organization on its Z- where it wants to be?
2. How clear is the organization on it's A- where it is today?
3. What are the turning points required to get where you want to be?

Bottom line: Is your organization moving quickly enough in driving the desired transformation?

CHAPTER THREE:

WHAT IS TRANSFORMATION?

In our discussions of Change Velocity, we will use the definition of transformation eluded to earlier: "a change in form, appearance, nature and character."

TRANSFORMATION ANALOGY

Consider the whole nature of transformation represented by a glass of cold iced tea. Lukewarm water transformed to cold cubes of ice. Sugar dissolved in the tea to transform the bitter liquid to sweet. There are multiple types of transformation to be seen in the glass of sweet tea:

- Transformation in form, bag of tea leaves to brown liquid.

- Transformation in appearance, white crystals of sugar that disappear into the liquid.
- Transformation in nature, bitter tea to sweet.

All these steps lead to the ultimate transformation in character. A cold glass of sweet tea on a hot summer day in Georgia can give me an all-new perspective, taking me from sweaty and disgruntled, to smiling and ready for my next challenge.

Types of Transformation

TRANSFORMATION IN FORM

While the transformation of tea bag to liquid tea may seem a bit far from the transformations you want to drive in your organization, let's move through the elements of the transformation and see what we can learn. Now, consider the tea bag itself. There is an aroma that creates a hint of things to come, the aroma you will soon be able to taste once the tea bag changes form. The principle in business is much the same: breathe in and catch a whiff of what is happening around you and your organization. I actually find this to be best to do with my eyes closed, as it suddenly sharpens your sense of smell and creates an opportunity to see the world for a few moments from our minds eye without the distraction of the visual world around us. As you think about the future state of your organization, take time to be quiet and reflect on what the organization will look like in the future. What form do you want it to take? What elements of that form currently exist in your organization? My experience today is that the immediate demands take our thoughts from the possibilities of the future. Remember to stop, smell the aroma of the tea, and read the tea leaves, so to speak. Transformation requires understanding both where we are and where we want to go, our current form and our desired form.

So, after having reflected on the aroma of the tea and the reading of the tea leaves, you should have a clear view of what is happening around you. Consider all aspects affecting the form your business takes and will take: What is happening with your customers? What is happening with your competition? Where is technology headed? How is the economic environment? What is happening in the political world? What new regulations are coming? What is happening with your customer's customers? How are the people doing in your own organization? In our work, we have found it useful to think about these external and internal influences that are impacting an organization and causing the need for change. We use a visual to represent these changes while taking the time to reflect on where the organization is and more importantly where the people in the organization are with regard to the influences that are driving the need for change. This is our opportunity to understand what is happening around us, as well as the impact on our organization.

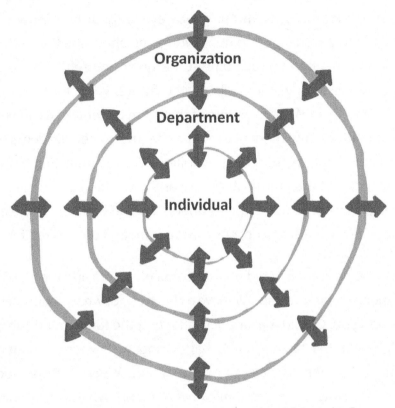

Internal and External Influences

With the simple laws of physics, we understand that for every action there is an equal and opposite reaction. As these influences put new external and internal pressures on your organization, what will your reactions be? On the other hand, what will happen if you choose to do nothing? What will be the impact of *no* reaction? One of my colleagues once asked me if inaction is action. While inaction may not be a deliberate action, inaction will create an organizational reaction. Have you ever heard that whisper around the office - don't "they" see what is happening? Something is happening, whether we take action or not. Another business colleague says that as a leader, "you can't say nothing". A lack of verbal comment carries a non-verbal communication. However, we may not be aware of the perceived message being transmitted throughout the organization. It might be the look on our face, the lack of eye contact, or lack of pep in our step. Saying nothing says something. If this is the case, we must take action when changes are occurring around us. As leaders, our teams expect us to show the way forward through the changes in markets, competition, business environment and political environment. A leader must know the current form of the organization so as to hold the current form while assessing the necessary changes that will create a change in form. Our goal should be to maintain and grow the momentum to help create the Change Velocity required for the business transformations today and in the future.

TRANSFORMATION IN APPEARANCE

The transformation of solid white sugar crystals to liquid represents a change in appearance. There are many other dramatic changes that we observe around us every day: a caterpillar becomes a butterfly, leaves turn to bright hues of red, yellow and orange in the fall weather, a flower sprouts from a bulb in the spring. The organizational transformations we seek are not always so obvious in appearance of transformation, but they should be. I have seen organizations acquire a totally new appearance. We worked on a project with a senior executive in the communications industry. The team of several hundred that he inherited in his new role were disheartened and bewildered in a continuing losing streak as the business continued to decline due to a number of internal and external influences. On the external front, consumer movement to mobile devices resulted in declining demand for fixed-line communications. New technologies such as calls through the Internet connections of personal computers resulted in declining profitability in the international calling segment. The quality differential had become less, with greater network bandwidth and speeds allowing for higher quality, internet-based calling. Competition from traditional and new competitors was eroding profit margins as the competition for the remaining business became even more intense. The water was boiling furiously, and the team could only see the hot water. This was the first task at hand, to change the perspective of possibility. To make matters worse, the group that provided the offerings sold through this indirect sales organization considered them competition for their primary direct sales force. The list of hurdles to success grew longer and longer with each conversation, as the new leader networked through the organization to get a sense of where the team was. Remember our discussion of understanding where you are, but always focusing on where you want to be.

The leader asked for our support in assessing where the organization was in order to determine a path forward, as his superiors expected them to turn the business around. After a number of interviews and discussions with team members, the picture was very clear. The group saw the continuing decline in the business as an irreversible market force that was outside of their control. We were asked to provide a motivating presentation at an upcoming all-hands meeting. How do you motivate a team that sees the game as unwinnable? As I pondered this request for several days, I considered turning down the assignment. However, this was a long-term executive level customer, so I took the job. At the presentation, I asked, "How good do you want to be?" and had them write this down on an index card. I then asked, "What must *you* do to be that good?" They wrote this on their index card as well. The emphasis was on the individual you, not the collective you of the organization. They then shared with a colleague their aspirations and how they planned to achieve them. Each pair became accountability partners, with required progress check-ins. The organization later recognized this as a real inflection point, when each individual became accountable. The appearance of the team changed as they achieved some internal and external wins. The wins were directly from the commitment cards that they had created in the session a few months before. There is something to be said for intrinsic motivation, when employees are on the path toward how good they as an individual want to be. The team simply needed motivation to transform their appearance to align with their nature. In my experiences, this intrinsic motivation is the real impetus for the change required for lasting transformation.

TRANSFORMATION IN NATURE

In our sweet tea analogy, the change in appearance, solid sugar to liquid, leads to a change in nature, from bitter tea to sweet. Both these changes are catalyzed by the hot water that melts the sugar. I find it very appropriate that hot, boiling water is required to create this transformation. This is very significant when you think about the reality of change in an organization. You frequently hear reference to the **burning platform** for change. The central idea is that an organization will not move without a real motivation to change. The burning platform could be new legal or regulatory requirements. It could be the result of changing macro-economic issues, or the result of a re-organization within the organization driven by mergers and acquisitions. A burning platform will create an impetus for change. However, there are many examples of burning platforms where the organization did not make the change required and ended up burned. Think of the effect of new delivery models like Netflix. There is no longer a demand for Blockbuster movie rentals or full cable services. The list goes on, examples of new business models driving out the old. New business models fueled by the sharing economy, such as Uber and AirBNB, change the way we think about taxi rides and hotel stays, changing the very nature of the way we think about these things. Or consider the new requirements for lending resulting from the Great Recession. These new regulations will shift the pattern of young buyers, with requirements for bigger down payments and more proof of capability to pay, leading young people to more often choose to pay rent in the city rather than buy a house in the suburbs like their parents.

Look for your boiling water, the impetus for change. And remember that others in your organization, your peers in other organizations, and even your entire industry will be experiencing their own boiling water moments. In the transformation of tea bags to sweet iced tea, boiling water creates the opportunity, not the result; the hand stirring the sugar into the hot water and then cooling the mixture appropriately creates the result. As we face the impetus for change and transformation, as leaders, we must change the perception of the hot water. The hot water is an opportunity to create something that will motivate your team, just as sweet tea can renew hope on a hot summer day. Leaders must focus on the potential of the hot water to create something good, rather than simply avoid it until it cools down. That is a key to accelerating change: recognizing the real opportunities.

The making of tea itself has experienced a transformation. While in the software business, I took many trips to Japan. On one such trip, I had the opportunity to enjoy a tea ceremony with Japanese friends. The Japanese tea ceremony maintains the rich tradition of drinking, enjoying and experiencing tea. They enjoyed sharing Japanese tradition and ways with me while finding humor in my ways. I shared with my host that I drank tea each and every morning at home at that time. They were fascinated, as the typical American beverage in the morning was coffee. They were further fascinated that a busy American businessman would take the time to prepare tea every morning. When I shared that it did not take so much time, as I simply took the cold iced sweet tea that my wife kept in the refrigerator, poured it into a mug, placed the mug in the microwave for two minutes, and then enjoyed my hot sweet tea. I will never forget the look of shock on their faces as they exclaimed, "That is not tea!" When you look around today at the various teas manufactured in bottles, the question becomes: is this new variety really tea? Or does the real essence of tea lie in the traditional experience of making and enjoying the tea? This is the same question asked every day as new approaches and innovations in business models, service models, products and social interactions change. What now is the norm? How has the nature of these things changed?

As a leader, it is important to not only understand the necessary changes in appearance, but also the nature of your team members who must make those changes. Asking for changes that go against their nature will be extremely difficult if the changes are counter to their core beliefs. In order for individuals to align their nature with a change, the leader must appeal to their nature in an attempt to create belief in the change. As you consider driving new change initiatives, remember that aligning the reason for the change and the expected actions with the nature or core beliefs of the team is essential to success in transformation. I saw a blog post just a few weeks back from another consulting firm where they were sharing about their experience starting up a business. I was surprised when they said that the team had met to discuss their values as a firm, but were having difficulty coming up with a statement of values. They asserted that when they saw it, they would know it. This concerned me, as it leads me to believe this firm will follow others blindly if they do not have a determined set of values. Writing down the values of an organization is critically important, but most important is living the values of the organization in such a way that they are demonstrated in your interactions with your colleagues, customers and suppliers. If your organization is having a hard time penning your values, it could be the leader is uncertain of their own values. Or there could be broad discrepancy in values across the organization, which is a major problem. Your customers and your colleagues will notice the discrepancy, which will create uncertainty and distrust. If your organization is having a challenge defining your values, or your nature, a great way to gain some perspective on the values that you are demonstrating is to ask your customers and suppliers. What are the core values they see demonstrated in your interactions? What is your appearance to those around you?

I want to leave you with **three questions** to consider as you look ahead to your next transformation initiative:

1. How well does the leadership team understand the meaning of transformation?
2. How committed is the leadership team to making sweet tea—initiating change in form, appearance, nature, *and* character?
3. How well does where you want to be align with the nature (core beliefs) of your team?

Bottom line: Is your leadership team ready to make transformation happen?

CHAPTER FOUR:

WHAT NEEDS TRANSFORMATION?

In this chapter, we will explore the elements of transformation and the required ingredients for success using an illustration of a pie. Before we begin our transformation pie discussion, however, let's first focus on what really needs to be transformed to successfully reach your desired state: attitude.

CHANGE ATTITUDE

You have probably heard the expression that attitude is everything. Or, hire for attitude and you can train the rest. Well, attitude is top of the list in leading an organizational transformation, both your attitude as the leader as well as your team's attitude. We worked with an associate for a few years who was always willing to try a new task or approach. I often think of him when considering organizational transformation, because his willingness to try something new enabled us to advance many change initiatives and innovations in our business. The other aspect of the personal change required that impacts the success of the transformation is the attitude of the individuals in the organization towards change. A willing attitude is ideal for timely and effective organizational transformation. I view willingness as the desire to try a new approach with a positive and curious perspective. A positive perspective is open to believing in the new approach; a curious perspective seeks to understand how the new way is different from and potentially better than the old way. A curious individual appreciates diverse approaches and enjoys the adventure of learning through the process of change. A willing individual focuses on the opportunities found in change, rather than the inconvenience of change. As the rate of change around us accelerates, the opportunities to learn are increasing as well. When deployed purposefully, transformational initiatives create a systematic approach for team learning. Rather than offering presentations about a required transformation, engage your team in the action and learning inherent in the transformation.

People, process and tools are often touted as key for driving a change. But without winning the hearts of your team, you will not have the willing people that are needed for success. Without their intellectual buy-in, they will not embrace the process. Without enabling, the tools are just tools. I have several electric drills sitting around in my utility room at home and haven't drilled a hole in years. My heart is not in it, as I do not get much joy or satisfaction in the use of a drill. Intellectually, I know that having a handy man do the drilling required around my house will result in a better quality of work. Last time I tried a drilling project myself, the drill bits that I selected would not penetrate the wood due to the wrong type of drill bit, discovered after hours of frustration. If I had only taken time to discuss the bit with the store associate when I picked them out. A little bit of advice and guidance could have been just the right enablement for me. Winning the hearts, winning the minds and enabling the change will get you the transformation you desire. More on winning hearts and creating believers in your transformation in Chapter Seven. For now, let's discuss the tools required for transformation.

Transformation Pie

SLICES OF TRANSFORMATION PIE

While transformational initiatives do require programmatic communication of the purpose, the reason for the changes, the roles of the individuals, the progress and the successes in the transformation, communication is only one slice of the transformation pie. Revelation, Determination, Communication, Acceleration, and Indication are the five slices of the transformation pie. Revelation—envisioning where you want to be; Determination—understanding where you are; Communication—making transformation information accessible to individuals in your organization; Acceleration—moving to where you want to be; Indication—understanding where you are and which direction you are moving in.

Revelation. Revelation is all about vision. When I hear about transformations, the descriptions are frequently of goals rather than visions. Goals tell us targets, but visions tell us how our organization will look and act differently after the transformation. How will customers or constituents view us differently? Something I have heard frequently in discussions with large global organizations is that their customers view them as difficult to do business with. Transformation is accomplished in an organization that is viewed as difficult to do business with when customers say the organization is easy to do business with. This should be the vision of the leaders of such organizations. So, what needs to change in your organization, and what is your vision, your idea of the difference the transformation will make? Vision is future-focused, it's about where you want to be. It communicates your purpose and what you value. The vision should inspire you and your team to give your best efforts.

Determination. Determination is about knowing where you are. What is your "A", your starting point? This slice of the pie is frequently the largest, the first place organizations want to focus. While that large slice of the pie can look appetizing, it can be overfilling. It is ineffective when an inordinate amount of the transformational strategy analysis focuses on a backward view of the business or situation, rather than a forward view of where you want to be and how to get there (the "Z"). I refer to this as the **First Slice Phenomenon.** If the first slice of pie is too large, the slices start getting smaller and smaller as the pie is consumed and, suddenly, the reality hits that there is not enough pie left to satisfy the requirements for effective transformation. As you consider allocating time and resources to the pieces of your transformational pie, remember the First Slice Phenomenon! Determination can be defined as "ascertainment, as after observation or investigation" (dictionary.com)* as well as "the quality of being resolute" (dictionary.com)*. Both definitions are integral to success in leading your organization through transformations as you ascertain where you are ("A") and resolve to move to where you want to be ("Z").

Communication. Communication is inevitable. You can't not communicate. That is a double negative, but, mathematically, two negatives make a positive, which means that you are always communicating. Inaction communicates, action communicates, words communicate, and lack of words communicates. Your organization is getting a message either formally or informally. Intentional transformation requires communication of a clear vision of where you want to go. What will the Promised Land look like? How will life be different and, more importantly, better in the Promised Land? I have used the word promise deliberately. As a leader communicating expectations of your vision, you make a commitment to do your part in making that vision a reality. You promise that something will be done and that you will do your part. Promise can also be "an indication of future excellence or achievement" (dictionary.com)*. This organization has great promise. This strategy has great promise. As we know from the many stories of the journey to the Promised Land, the reality is that the journey isn't without its challenges and setbacks. From the right perspective, however, a setback is an opportunity for growth. As you lead transformation, there will be setbacks. Your role is to lead the organization to the comebacks from those setbacks through a continued focus on the Promised Land. This will require communication of the vision, communication of the setbacks and communication of the comebacks.

Acceleration. Acceleration is about increasing velocity. How quickly can the organization move from A to Z, from where you are to where you want to be? Change Velocity is the time to change the direction of an organization or individual to align with a desired transformation. As we have setbacks, we must continuously focus the direction back toward the Promised Land to remind the organization of the vision. This direction of individuals requires communication. Communication exists in many forms today, from one-on-one discussions, to small group meetings, to internal media dissemination through webcast/podcast/visual story telling. It is important to consider the frequency and form of communication to align with the audience and purpose of the communication. Velocity is about both speed and direction. Consider the direction of activity in your organization—what is the organization focused on? Are you focused on the right markets, customers, activities and actions to move in the right direction? (You may be wondering—what is the difference between activities and actions? More on that in Chapter Five.)

Indication. Indication is about measuring progress. Validating the focus, activities, and actions on a regular cadence can be time consuming and potentially not very scalable for a leader of a large organization. An organization needs an adequate indication of where they are in order to determine whether they are driving the right activities. If the indicators, the measurements of progress, are clearly understood by the organization, this will allow for self-adjustment among employees, thereby accelerating the journey to the Promised Land. This is a major failing of most transformational initiatives, the lack of future-oriented indicators. We certainly need goals, as they will provide opportunities for measuring progress. Moving from a lagging view of progress focused on the past to a leading view of progress focused on the future is the major shift required in the role of indication in organizational transformation. There is a substantial set of information about yesterday's results, last week's results, last month's results, last quarter's results, year to date results and last year's results. The ability to capture, report and analyze results is less of an issue today with point of interaction capture capabilities resulting from the connectivity of the world. The real issue is capturing the right information that is a **leading indicator** of what will happen, as opposed to a **lagging indicator** based on what happened in the past. More about leading and lagging indicators in Chapter Five.

INGREDIENTS IN THE TRANSFORMATION PIE

Now that we know the slices of the transformation pie, let's look at the ingredients making up these pieces of pie. A slice of pie without the right ingredients just doesn't taste that good! Do you have the right ingredients to create that good tasting pie? The ingredients of the transformation pie are: Leading, Inquiring, Persisting, Motivating and Measuring.

Leading. Leading is required for any transformation. Frequently, decisions to change fall into the black hole of indecision, and indecision becomes the decision without anyone realizing it. Leading is required to create momentum for movement. Someone has to stand up and take the first step or push hard enough for the change to drive the transformation. Taking a leadership role in transformation can be either a conscious proactive action or a reactive action. Someone with strong awareness of new influences in the market, as well as changes in customers and competition may set a new vision or course for the organization proactively. Likewise, in the heat of battle, leaders often emerge within teams as organizations focus on how to survive. Leading is about showing the way through thoughts and actions. Who is leading transformation in your organization?

Inquiring. Inquiring minds are curious and seek to understand. Critical to the process of inquiring is also deliberating. Discussion of various questions and perspectives will lead to a greater understanding for each person involved. How many questions are being generated in your organization to better understand what is happening around you.? Are you building that culture of curiosity by encouraging the Curious Whys?

Persisting. Persisting is all about staying power, willingness to stay focused on where you want to be. Many people fail not because of a poor strategy or vision, but for lack of persistence in action and activity to drive toward the desired results. It takes many single steps to reach a mountain peak, but you will never reach it if you do not keep moving in the right direction. Do you and your organization have the persistence to stay the course?

Motivating. Motivating is about creating an intrinsic push toward where you want your team to be. You must energize people to reach the Promised Land, the "Z". As we look to create the push and pull through internal and external motivation, always remember the power of belief. Belief and understanding (heart and mind) will be important factors in generating the intrinsic motivation. As the leader, you must also ensure that the external rewards and recognition align with the desired changes for the transformation. Does the team believe in the destination and the means of getting there? Does the team understand the reality of where you currently are?

Measuring. Measuring is about understanding progress. We must understand where we are as a baseline to measure progress toward our goals. Measurement has a cause and effect that must be understood. Many examples exist of measurement and the behavioral impact. If you require a certain number or amount of opportunities in a salesperson's pipeline you may get the quantity, but not the quality of opportunities; if you require a certain quality of opportunities in terms of specific criteria, you may not get the same quantity of opportunities. The opportunity and potential to measure is greater than ever due to Rapid Dissemination. So, the issue may not be how to measure, but rather what to measure.

With the ability to collect and measure more information, the real skill is in ensuring that the right information is being collected. Is the information measured in alignment with the operational and behavioral actions that the organization wants to drive to support the organization changes?

With the transformation pie properly baked with the right ingredients (Leading, Inquiring, Persisting, Motivating and Measuring), and sliced appropriately to avoid the First Slice Phenomenon, you will be on your way to enjoying each and every slice (Revelation—envisioning where you want to be; Determination—understanding where you are; Communication—making transformation information accessible to individuals in your organization; Acceleration— moving toward your goal; Indication—understanding where you are and which direction you are moving in). A properly baked and sliced transformation pie should taste good to your team and have you looking like a master transformation chef!

I want to leave you with **three questions** as you consider what needs to be transformed in your organization:

1. How will you proactively create the right slices for your transformation pie? (Revelation, Determination, Communication, Acceleration, Indication)
2. How will you ensure the right ingredients are in place?
3. How will you avoid the First Slice Phenomenon?

Bottom line: Does your leadership team understand what really needs to be transformed?

CHAPTER FIVE:

FROM STRATEGY TO EXECUTION

The accelerated pace of change in the business environment requires a greater focus on the iterative process for creating a closed loop connection between strategy and execution. Too many organizations focus on strategy but fail to execute their strategy. The strategy must be sensitive to the many changes impacting an organization's ability to execute the strategy. These changes are driven by market influences such as competitors, customers, suppliers, and innovators. All these influences likewise create new demands on the leadership responsible for driving execution of strategies.

The secret to moving from strategy to execution lies in three areas:

1. Make the strategy digestible: Is it clear for the organization where you want to go?

2. Understand your business model: Does the organization understand the key levers?
3. Define the leading indicators: Do we know if we are moving in the right direction?

You may think there is more to it than one, two, three. You are right. The usual operational things need to happen around your strategy communication plan and cadence, like the measuring of results and adapting based on feedback. The feedback loop is critical in driving strategy to execution. The three most common issues we see as organizations strive to move from strategy to execution are:

1. The strategy is unclear or misunderstood by the organization
2. The lagging indicator metrics are not change actionable
3. The responsiveness of the organization is slow due to lagging vs. leading indicators

LEADING VS. LAGGING INDICATORS

If your organization struggles to execute, it is time to slow down and reflect on your leading indicators. Many organizations keep moving, seeking to catch up with the demands of the changing market, but with no vision. The traditional lagging indicators were adequate in calmer times with fewer and slower changes, but leading indicators are critical in the environment of accelerating change today. In my experience with clients, leading indicators are not always so apparent without a clear understanding of the cause and effect relationships within a business. This cause and effect relationship requires a peeling back of the results to see the actions that drive the result. We worked with a client with an inside/outside sales team coverage model. There was one inside sales representative teamed with three field sales representatives. When the new model was implemented, the role-specific activities were analyzed to understand what level of activity was required to achieve the target results for each team. We asked questions around numbers of calls and numbers of visits required to win a new account or expand within an existing account. From the start of this analysis, the obvious impact of quality of activity became very apparent as the numbers varied based on the effectiveness of the sales interactions, which can be a skill issue as well as a customer fit issue. Were the sales teams doing the right quantity of activities? Were they focused on the right accounts? Were they delivering quality services? As we explored these questions, the organization tuned the quantity, focused on the right target customers, and improved the quality of their services. The results for the organization improved dramatically as they focused on their new account acquisition strategy. The company moved from #2 in share to #1 in market share over a three-year period due to the impact of the new account acquisition strategy. Other factors, such as motivation, drove this successful initiative as well. The initial compensation plan deployed with the new account acquisition roles was not aligned with the behavior desired, which was a "land and expand" strategy. Land the new account, get the contracting vehicles for the core set of solutions in place with a buying portal, then expand through up-sell and cross-sell activities. The shift to a compensation plan that recognized the first most critical step in this strategy—landing the account—was a move from the traditional focus on revenue only.

Organizational leaders must have a future-oriented view. If it were as simple as visiting the palm reader to see the future, fewer leaders would have restless nights as they struggle for sustainable growth and profitability with shorter runways to success. This desire to predict the future has resulted in the many solutions being promoted in the business community for harnessing the power of analytics and harnessing the power of the ever-bigger data. I recently participated in a roundtable meeting with senior sales executives. A key topic was simplifying the number of metrics captured so the metrics being captured are actually helpful. It sounds simple, but it's easier said than done. In our work with hundreds of sales leaders, we have found that the focus in the sales reviews as well as the individual team discussions is most often centered around the forecast for the month and the quarter. Where is the business year to date and where do they expect to be for the year? The discussions rarely focus on the ever-important leading indicators. Are they doing what is necessary to drive the desired results? I frequently hear discussion about the sales pipeline relative to items in the 30, 60 and 90-day pipelines of opportunity. While it potentially lures us into some comfort speaking about the distant 90-day future, these metrics are actually a lagging indicator. Our pipeline of sales opportunity as it exists at any minute is a snapshot of results from the past. Marketing events, social media activity, cold calls, referrals, and networking activities result in a sales pipeline; the current quantity and quality of opportunities reflect these past activities. In order to shift to a future-focus, you as a leader must ask two questions. What actions and activities will advance the current opportunities in the pipeline? What actions and activities will generate new opportunities entering the pipeline?

ACTIONS AND ACTIVITIES

I realize that I have used in the prior sentence and in the prior paragraphs the terms actions and activities. You may be asking what the difference is. **Actions** are in response to a specific situation. So, we go to the doctor and learn that we are overweight and in poor physical condition. Our first action is to go to the gym for an assessment of our fitness to determine a workout routine that is best for us. **Activities** are actions executed on a repeatable basis. When we execute the workout routine on a recurring basis, we have moved from action to activity. When our day feels empty when we have not done the activity, we have established the habit. Situation to Action to Activity to Habit.

The complexity and size of organizations has moved people further from the actions and activities involved in running the organizations. When you have a small business and are running it day to day, you intuitively understand the business model, as you are involved in all aspects of operation. You are familiar with the actions of your business because you frequently perform them. You know that without sales there will be no business. You know that without delivering value for the customers, there will be no repeat business. You know the effort to gain a new customer is high and costly as compared to selling more to an existing customer. The time from action and activity to result is small as you are on the front line. You feel the result as bank balances go up or down and customers come or go. As organizations grow, the understanding of the business model and the cause and effective relationships get lost in the requisite specialization that occurs. You see it very clearly in comments you hear around an organization, such as:

"Why do sales people make so much?" (Implementation team discussing sales team)

"Why can't operations deliver on the customer's orders?" (Sales team discussing operations)

"Why is service so slow?" (Operations and sales discussing service)

"Why does product development and launch take so long?" (Sales, operations and services discussing product development)

You get the message. If you understand the business model, many of the answers to these questions are clear. More importantly, with the right leading indicators in place, you proactively adapt rather than reacting to the situation based on lagging indicators. We often hear the statement from clients and prospective clients that their business is complex, not a simple transactional business where you can relate an action and activities to a result. Regardless of the business complexity, it is a law of physics and a law of business: for every action there is a reaction. It is even more important to understand these relationships in a complex business, as the complexity masks the real actions that are the levers in driving the results. If you do not know the levers in your business, invest the time to discover them.

Just a few clarifications relative to the "why" questions above. I have these in italics to be representative of what I refer to as the Whiney Whys. The Whiney Whys exist in a dysfunctional organization. However, I am a big believer in the **Curious Whys**. The curious whys drive the organization to look deeply at the business interrelationships and facilitate the cause & effect thinking required in the Business Model Approach. Let's consider a few examples of curious whys. Curious whys seek to understand more deeply the situation, the business and all of the key levers in the business.

- Why are we growing so quickly?
- Why are we not growing faster?
- Why enter this market vs. other markets?
- Why is this service team so productive?
- Why is this service team unproductive?
- Why are our costs higher that the competition?
- Why are our costs lower than the competition?
- Why is our new product introduction process so long?

Most curious why questions are a simple construct, but powerful in cutting to the core of the situation. The tone of delivery of a curious why also has an impact. The delivery of the question is all focused on greater understanding, rather than accusation. Another bit of advice is to have multiple ways to ask why. Now, why would that matter? Well, about three whys in a row may get a little irritating for the person trying to produce the answers. All parents have probably heard the many curious whys of a toddler. After three curious questions in a row, we may just want to say, "because that's the way it is!" Interlacing with a few other ways of asking the Curious Why will allow us to get to the root cause of the issue without alienating the person that needs to provide the answer. This will create more of a dialogue as compared to an inquisition. You may also try re-framing some of your questions without using the word 'why,' but using 'what' or 'how' instead.

- Why are we growing so fast in this market?

- What factors are impacting our growth in this market?
- How can we replicate this growth in additional markets?

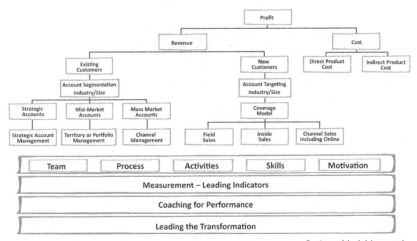

Business Model Approach

BUSINESS MODEL APPROACH

We use the **Business Model Approach** to help organizations shift to thinking about the interactions of cause & effect with how the business makes money. Yes, the Business Model Approach focuses on how the business makes money, but more importantly, it focuses on what key levers can be used to improve profitability in the business. The second key principle of the Business Model Approach is a focus on leading indicators. At the top of the Business Model, where much of the reporting, analysis and projections typically focus, are the results, or the profit—revenue minus cost. For our purposes, we will focus on the Revenue dimension of the cause and effect chain, as our discussions in this book are primarily on sales transformation. Clearly, there are decisions around revenue that effect cost, which include go-to-market approach by direct sales or channel, industry or cross industry focus, inside or field sales representatives, compensation, and many more. Revenue generation is the purpose of sales. When looking at revenue and contributors to revenue, we simply ask where the revenue comes from. In the example we will explore, we have sources of revenue from both existing customers and new customers. For existing customers, we ask how we want to segment our customers in terms of industry, size and geography. Based on current business and potential, we have three segments of accounts: Strategic accounts, Mid-Market Existing accounts, and Smaller Mass Market accounts. Based on our decisions regarding account segmentation, our next decision will be to cover these accounts in each segment and generate the best results using five leverage factors: Team, Process, Activities, Skills and Motivation.

Integral to the Business Model Approach is the focus on identification and measurement of leading indicators. Let's explore this topic of leading indicators across our five leverage factors.

TEAM:

Do we have the right roles (Sales Leadership, Sales, Pre-Sales Support, Post-Sales Support) on the team to successfully address the customer segment?

- Does each role have the right knowledge, skills and attributes for success?
- Do we have leading indicators in place to determine if we have the right knowledge, skills and attributes for success?

PROCESS:

- What is the customer engagement process for the customer segment?
- How effective is the customer engagement process?
- What are the leading indicators for an effective customer engagement?

ACTIVITIES:

- Which activities are the "key activities"?
- What are the expected results for these key activities?
- How will we measure these key activities that lead to the key results?

SKILLS:

- What skills are currently in place across the team?
- Where do we need to improve skills?
- Which skills support the key activities required to accomplish the key results?

MOTIVATION:

- How motivated is the team?
- How can we increase motivation?
- What are the leading indicators for motivation?

The good news is that as a result of Rapid Dissemination, Faster Creation and Time To, collecting, measuring and providing feedback on these five leverage factors is now a reality. We work with one client using gaming technology to create engagement and motivation for the sales force. Other clients are serving up automated customer engagement and process tips to the sales representatives' mobile devices. Proximity of information to the point of customer engagement creates new opportunities for enabling processes and approaches with the opportunity to capture immediate feedback. As you consider your own organizational transformation, identify the levers and the key leading indicators (frequently called KPIs—Key Performance Indicators) across the five leverage factors that will ensure you are moving in the right direction. When working with clients, we frequently find the most challenging part of the Business Model Approach is defining and prioritizing the Key Performance Indicators.

I started my career as a finance and accounting professional, then moved into technology sales, then sales leadership and marketing leadership roles, with a touch of product development and field operations along the way. So this thinking around business model, metrics, and looking for the root cause took me back to discussions of activity-based accounting and variance analysis during my cost accounting days. Cost accounting requires a deep understanding of the production process, the interrelationship of materials, labor and inputs to the production process plus related indirect cost such as facilities and utilities that are required for production of the product. It very much requires cause-and-effect thinking with respect to identifying the inputs, the outputs, and the related elements of cost.

When our team at SOAR spoke with executives about teaching their sales leaders, directors and managers about their business model, the executives often wondered if leaders, directors, and managers would care, and if it would be worth the time and investment to teach them. Our response to these questions centered on the importance of driving sustainable and repeatable profitability. The sales roles are critical for that success, and a change in thinking from lagging to leading indicators is integral to repeatable, predictable revenues and profits. You may ask why it is important for the sales roles to clearly understand the business model. Many decisions made during the customer interactions of the sales cycle have dramatic impact on the effectiveness of the overall business model. For example, if our service approach is a low touch self-service model, it is important for this to be clear for the customer during the sales engagement. If our primary lead product is low margin due to a highly competitive market and up-sell/cross-sell activities are critical for profitability, the sales team must understand this business model in order to effectively execute the strategy. If cash flow is critical to the business, understanding the impact of extended payment terms is important. Certainly, many of these items can be addressed in compensation plans to reinforce or discourage specific actions. However, the business model approach is all about getting your sales team and other teams to think like business *owners*. How do my actions, activities and behaviors impact my company and the customers? Regardless of the complexity of a business, it is a law of physics and a law of business: for every action there is a reaction. It is even more important to understand these relationships in a complex business as the complexity masks the real actions that are the levers in driving the results. If you do not know the levers in your business, invest the time to discover them. The learning process will be a transformational experience. The amazing part of our work with the business model is how the thinking starts to permeate the broader organization from sales to service to operations to finance when the leaders start to ask about those leading indicators in the daily interactions. Remember, the answers you get are in the questions you ask. Those very same incisive questions will lead to the actions and ultimately the activities that create the habits of success.

Does this shift in thinking from lagging indicators to leading indicators really matter? More importantly, does it work? The answer is yes and yes. We led an effort with a client that was initially focused on the country sales directors and later focused on the top talent sales managers. The initial wave of the deployment in the organization resulted in over $250 million in increased revenue in a very competitive market. This was very substantial for a then $2 billion business. The focus on action and activities to drive the levers in the business created the mind shift that supported the transformation. The reality is, intellectually, organizations get it. We know we need to focus on actions and activities that drive the results. The problem is that lagging metrics associated with our traditional financial reporting are predominant in the business world. The most forward-looking view aligns with the monthly and quarterly financial views of the future required for most organizations' reporting. Actions and activities that drive those results are deeper in the cause and effect tree of the business model. What are the drivers of revenue results? What actions and activities impact those results? As we move through the cause and effect tree, this is where we will finally discover the actions and activities that will lead to the result. The good news about actions and activities is that we can choose them. We choose to take the action, choose to repeat the activity, and then we can relate the activities to a result. We may choose to target a new type of prospective customer, then choose to drive five touches for each prospective customer over a

30-day period. We can then measure the results of our action and activities. Are we seeing increases in the numbers of prospective customers engaging with us? Are we turning that engagement into opportunities? How are those opportunities progressing?

The Closed Loop from strategy to execution consists of four elements: Action, Activity, Measurement and Refinement. The Closed Loop is an internal feedback loop. What action (first step) will we take? How will we turn the action into repeatable activities? What are the priority activities? How will we measure the activities from a quantity and quality perspective? What will be our process for refining our activities and defining new actions based on the results of measurement? Ironically, the very same Rapid Dissemination, Faster Creation and Time To demands that place external pressure on your organization will also enable you to improve this closed loop. Rapid Dissemination provides for a more rapid feedback of information. Faster Creation allows for the rapid development and deployment of closed loop feedback systems, process improvements and new approaches. Time To has created a focus on understanding the time to do any action and activity, which will lead to a result. The hurdles for capturing actions and activities that drive the results across an organization from sales to service to operations were restrictive in the past due to the high cost of collecting, analyzing, and accessing the information. Rapid Dissemination, Faster Creation and Time To are catalyst for this ability for accelerating the closed loop approach. In my experience, the shift toward closing the loop all started in manufacturing almost 40 years ago as organizations sought to get feedback from the factory floor to business systems. We now see it in utilities where meters are read remotely and feed information for billing purposes. We see it in our homes, with remote control thermostats and security systems that can be managed remotely through mobile phones.

Organizations benefiting from this new found closer connection to the action and activities will be those that employ cause and effect focused business model thinking. The time and energy to focus on the business model pays benefits by helping the organization understand those leading indicators and the associated actions and activities that provide leverage for the business. While the barriers between departments of a business have been lessened, the reality is that the shift in thinking from lagging to leading indicators is required in parallel with implementation of this closed loop. The hurdles for this shift in thinking will be high with the litigious culture of today, which has resulted in bold print on most financial statements. The investment and financial rules even discourage the forward view with the large disclaimers at the start of any financial presentation. Companies are forced to over-explain the fact that their projections are subject to uncertainties outside their control, and they are thus not liable for anything causing their forward view to be thwarted. A focus on understanding the current situation is important as you understand where you are as an input to where you want to go. The focus on transparency for financial and public information is a good thing. But, a future view for where you want to go is critical for leading transformation and creating Change Velocity. Otherwise, an organization is just in a constant state of "in-process" and as everyone experienced with process improvement knows, in-process is costly, as there is no opportunity to recognize value until it is complete. This only amplifies the call for Change Velocity in moving from where your organization is to where you want to be.

I want to leave you with **three questions** to consider as you move from strategy to execution:

1. How well does your organization understand the business model and the cause & effect tree?
2. How will you create the closed loop from Action to Activities to Measures to Refinement?
3. How are you creating a focus on those curious whys for your organization?

Bottom line question for you: Does your organization understand the key levers that will drive the results?

CHAPTER SIX:

CREATING CHANGE VELOCITY

In Chapter Two, we defined Change Velocity as the time to change the direction of an organization or individual to align with a desired transformation. We also discussed the importance of understanding your "A" as well as your "Z"—where you are and where you want to be. We will focus in this chapter on how to create Change Velocity. But how does your organization go from "A" to "Z"? The first step as we discussed may be simply the movement from A to B. Starting the journey is important, but as discussed with the rapid rate of change in the market, the real issue is how to lead an organizational transformation that leads to more organizational transformations.

Accelerating the rate of change in position of an organization in a specified "new" direction relies on three variables.

1. Change View
2. Change Reaction
3. Change Motivation

CHANGE VIEW

A **Change View** can be considered at three levels: the overall organization, a part of the organization or an individual. Consider the cause and effect aspects of the business model discussed in Chapter Five. The organization is made up of various functional departments, and the departments are made of individuals. When you consider the contagious nature of attitude, it is easy to see how a department or entire organization can be substantially impacted by the Change View of a specific individual. When we look at Change View, there are typically 3 predominant views. You can think of them as a continuum.

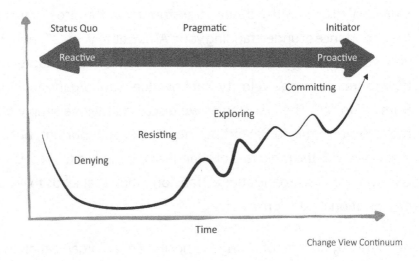

Change View Continuum

On the left side are individuals who prefer the world the way it is. This is referred to as Status Quo Change View. Now, why do they prefer the status quo? They are making good money, have a good work life balance, have a good boss, work at a great company. Alternatively, they may make okay money, have an okay work life balance, have an okay boss, work for an okay company. Regardless, they are satisfied with the current situation, preferring it to the risk, uncertainty and potential rewards encompassed in a change. Status Quo Change View tends not to see or think about where they could be, the 'Z' possibilities. This group is best in an environment with incremental change, gradual and continuous improvement. This group engages in the Curious Whys, such as: Why do we need to change? Why such a big change? Why now? I worked at a software company when Microsoft introduced Windows. The Vice President for product development was a Unix expert who perceived Unix as the industrial-strength operating system. After taking an initial look at Windows, it was concluded that it was just a new technology fad that would take time to become industrial strength and for adoption in the market. What was not anticipated was the rapid adoption of Windows through the marketing power and partnerships of Microsoft. In about four years, the software company that I worked at which had been a leader in its market was no longer relevant in the market. Companies that embraced the Windows operating system surpassed the company because of massive adoption of Windows in the market place driven by Microsoft. When Google hit the market, how do you think this search engine was perceived? How is it perceived today?

These examples highlight the impact of a Status Quo Change View. The world is changing with us or without us. The difference is that the result of Rapid Dissemination, Faster Creation and Time To is a world that is changing ever more quickly with us or without us. In several working sessions with clients on leading innovation, I have been asked whether there is room for the Status Quo Change View today. If we consider Change View to be part of an individual's nature, and if we assume an equal distribution of people in the world with one of the three Change Views, then there is a 33.3% chance that an individual has a Status Quo Change View. So, in this case, the issue is not whether there is a place for Status Quo Change View, but how we deal with those individuals and move them through the changes in our organizations. We will spend more time on this topic of moving individuals through the change as we dive into the topic of Change Reaction.

Now, look to the far right on the continuum and see the Initiator Change View. Individuals with this view prefer faster and more radical change. They will frequently challenge the existing structure. This group engages in different Curious Whys, such as: Why do we do it that way? Why are we organized this way? I am often asked in sessions on innovation whether it is best to have an organization filled with Initiatiors in these times of accelerating change in the market. With the same 33.3% probability someone will have an Initiator Change View, is this likely to happen? When you look at the Initiator Change View, it becomes very clear that faster and more radical change have both a potential value and a potential cost. For example, how important is an Initiator likely to perceive a small, but potentially important change in expense reporting procedures to satisfy new accounting regulations, as compared to creating a new game changing go-to-market strategy? Again, the important point is to recognize that employees will have different Change

Views. Leaders must understand their own Change View and the Change View of their team in order to support the acceleration of the movement from A to Z. Now, with some perspective on each end of the continuum, let's look at the center of the continuum, the Pragmatic Change View. The Pragmatic is willing to explore the existing situation in an open and objective manner, advocating change that aligns with the current situation. Their interest is in what will work. Pragmatics engage in the Curious Whys, such as: Will this change work? How will it work? Does it fit my customers, my role, my experiences and my view of the current situation? Applying our 33.3% odds, you are probably dealing with a few Pragmatics in your organization.

CHANGE REACTION

Let's move next to the topic of **Change Reaction**. While all of us have a Change View that is part of our nature, we have an individual Change Reaction for each specific change we encounter. Change Reaction has 4 phases: Denying the Need for Change, Resisting the Change, Exploring the Change and Committing to the Change. If we think of these as occurring sequentially over a period of time, then the real issue, regardless of the initial Change View of an individual or organization, is how quickly an individual can move through their Change Reaction. Another question that comes out frequently in change and innovation working sessions with clients is this: Will Initiators move more quickly through the Change Reaction than Status Quo or Pragmatic Change Views? Not necessarily. The reason is that the perceived importance of the change to the individual impacts the embrace of a change regardless of their Change View. If you have a room filled with top performing sales professionals who are all Initiators, you can tell them that they need to start filling out a new expense format for all of their travel expenses to meet new company expense reporting guidelines. How quickly do you think they will embrace this change? My estimate is that, left to choose when to adopt on their own, the adoption will be slow. There are systematic ways to encourage compliance such as not paying expenses unless they comply with the new format, but an Initiator is likely not enthused to adopt this change, as it is not perceived as game-changing to them. They may see the need for change, but need encouragement in the phase of Committing to the Change. Unsurprisingly, the Status Quo Change View requires the most encouragement in moving through the phases of Change Reaction. They are more likely to spend time in the first phase, Denying the Need for Change. If you convince them of the need by putting more effort in on the front end, they will move more quickly through the other phases. Now, what does moving through Change Reaction look like for the Pragmatic Change View? Imagine you believe you have a great idea, but you have not been able to quantify the real benefit to the team or the individuals on the team. How will the Pragmatics respond to this change? Remember, they need to see the benefit to them and they need to see how it relates to their current situation. In our work, we frequently observe changes and new approaches being introduced to pragmatics in an organization without the required proof for their view of change. If you do not have proof that it works, how will the Pragmatics test the validity of the new approach or change against their current situation? Pragmatics are more likely to spend time in the phase of Exploring the Change as they move through Change Reaction. So, each Change View requires different time and attention in each phase of the Change Reaction. Knowing how your team views change will enable you to effectively work with them as they react to change.

CHANGE MOTIVATION

After considering our first two variables, Change View and Change Reaction, let's move to the topic of Change Motivation. Change Motivation has two important dimensions: the logical and the emotional. We like to refer to this as winning the hearts and minds of the organization. To consider the amount of energy that goes into the logical dimension of motivation, you need only search online for topics like compensation. There is a continuous focus in change initiative conversations on how compensation can impact the embrace of change. In working with organizations on initiatives with their sales teams, I have heard comments about sales people being "coin-operated". Meaning, if you want them to do it, you must pay them to do it. It's true that money matters to sales professionals, as many are in the career because of the ability to earn more variable compensation through success in the sales role. However, I have often seen that many successful sales professionals see the compensation as a *by-product* of their success in selling, rather than their *motivation* for selling. There is nothing wrong with having great compensation plans to motivate performance, but consider the other intrinsic motivational factor that drives a sales professional: recognition. Recognition as #1 on the leaders' board, recognition through sales awards trips, recognition through positive customer feedback, recognition through praise from the executives in the company, the list goes on. Get creative in the ways you recognize members of your team. The real key is to understand that motivation is a combination of internal and external factors that we can dial-in to influence the embrace of change.

A question that is easy to ask, but not always easy to answer relative to a change is how life will be better for the individual after the change is implemented. Just as important to understand is how life will be better for the organization overall or for the specific department that is impacted by the change. In truth, the impact of a change all lies in the perspectives of the individuals, departments and organizations impacted. Earlier in my career, I worked with a software company that oversold our ability to deliver what customers expected as the result of missteps in the product development and delivery. There was a big gap in customer expectations set by the sales teams based on the product delivery plans and the reality of the product delivery from a timing as well as quality perspective. The result was a need to right-size the organization in order to survive the fall-out of slowing sales, upset customers and a general organizational crisis. It was one of the most difficult times in my professional career. Now, we all know the impact of right sizing is a reduction in force. I was tasked with having conversations with what seemed like an endless flood of people to inform them that they were either staying or being laid off. My job in this time of change was to let them know what would be better or different about their future, whether at that company or elsewhere. The best of the 'better' situations was that you got to keep your job working in product development and delivery…in a very difficult environment with a number of very upset customers with missed expectations. Or you got to keep your job in sales…to compete in a market with very aggressive competitors with our reputation that was not so good in terms of product delivery at the time. For the ones who received the message that their futures would be different, they heard that their position was being eliminated so the company could survive. Many of them sensed the inevitable, but they still couldn't believe the situation. They had been working in what at the time was considered a hot software start-up in a hot market with a hot new product coming out. The terms right sizing, reduction in force, and layoffs have become common expressions of our times that reflect organizations' inability to read the tea leaves effectively through a focus on leading indicators. In this case, these layoffs were better for the organization as it survived and ultimately thrived again, but not necessarily better for the individuals that lost jobs or were stressed by demands after the change.

Sometimes, however, what is best for the organization is also best for the individual. I have experienced a number of situations where an individual was not the right fit for a job. I can take responsibility for the hiring process in these cases, as the individuals worked for me. In one of these situations, I hired a very successful implementation consultant who had interest in technology sales into a technical pre-sales role with a software company. He had a great attitude, he had the knowledge of the solutions, he had the knowledge of the focus customers and he had the willingness to work hard to be successful. To our amazement, the ability to bring it all together in terms of the conversation in front of the customer was a struggle. We worked the issue, coached, practiced and finally concluded after several months that it wasn't going to work in our business environment. I will never forget sitting down to discuss the situation with this enthusiastic, committed individual. When I started the conversation, he immediately jumped in and shared how relieved he was. He had thought moving from service to technical sales would be a straight-forward evolution but found out that was not the case. Then it hit me that for this individual, it would be both different and better for him to move back to a role better suited for him, as he would no longer be stressed about his inability to meet the expectations of our business. I learned a very important lesson in this discussion: "better" is a relative term. I did not see letting this person go as something that would be better for him. However, it gave him the opportunity for success in a different role, which he found. It also meant a better situation for the organization and the regional sales team.

As you focus on creating Change Velocity, three factors will be at play, Change View, Change Reaction and Change Motivation. There is a multiplier effect associated with the interactions of these factors. Meaning that our ability as leaders to understand our teams Change View, Change Reaction and Change Motivation will be critical to creating this multiplier. Is the Change View: Status Quo, Pragmatic or Initiator? Where is the team in their Change Reaction: Denying, Resisting, Exploring or Committing? What is the Motivation to Change: Low, Medium or High? Do they see how life will be better or different after the change?

TRANSFORMATION GROUPS

Understanding the factors that will impact Change Velocity can help us in tailoring our communication strategy and engagement approach to the dynamics of the team. Also understanding who will make the transformation is important for leading a sales transformation. How can you identify who will likely make it in a sales transformation? In the end, it will be all about who can adopt the behaviors required for success in the new organization. Indicators such as Change View, Change Reaction, and Change Motivation can help you discern how individuals and departments will engage with the change. But there are two additional critical questions to consider when thinking about who will make the transition:

1. Is a team member *willing* to execute the new behaviors required for success?
2. Is a team member *capable* of executing the new behaviors required for success?

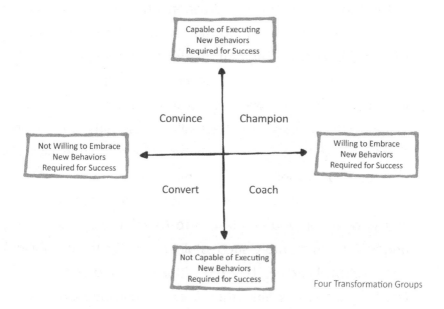

Four Transformation Groups

As a leader, you will have 4 groups within any transformation:

1. *Those who are Willing and Capable.* As a leader, you must **Champion** these individuals. To do this, you can recognize, reward and lift these people up in the organization. For example, in a project we recently worked on, one of the sales

managers in the organization fit this profile perfectly. He embraced the new, more strategic sales approach and was very capable of managing his team to execute it. His leader, being very savvy, gave him special projects to work on as a part of the transformation, recognized him as a leader throughout the organization and as a result of his team's performance, he later received a promotion.

2. *Those who are Capable, but not Willing.* As a leader, you must **Convince** these team members that embracing the new behaviors is to their benefit. Typically, these are individuals who have a long history of success and are invested in the status quo. We ran into this situation when recently working with a client. He has sold more in his lifetime than most people ever will, and convincing him that he needed to do anything differently was a tall task. However, the leadership team we were partnering with was able to show him that embracing some new behaviors would actually enable him to be even more successful. Ultimately, he became one of the role models championed throughout the organization.

3. *Those who are Willing, but not Capable.* As a leader, the best course of action you can take is to **Coach** these individuals and help them be more successful. Sometimes the capability gaps are small and can be fixed with a few good one-on-one coaching sessions, while other times the gaps are larger and require a more formal approach, such as training.

4. *Those who are not Willing and not Capable.* As a leader, you must **Convert** those in this group. Sometimes that means moving them into new roles within the company where they can be successful. Sometimes there simply isn't a role within the

organization where they can succeed and they will need to find new opportunities outside your organization.

As a leader in driving change that will move your organization through the transformation required to reach your end goal, who will you need to Champion, Convince, Coach or Convert? When you consider Change Velocity, it is critical to quickly assess where you are in order to then focus on how to drive the change. Where will you focus your time and the time of your team to create the greatest impact on Change Velocity? The time invested across the organization will be impacted by the effort invested in Championing, Convincing, Coaching and Converting of specific team members. A strategy we use with organizations is to quickly identify those that you want to Champion, having them take an active role in demonstrating the value of the change through their actions, activities and ultimately results. These examples of success provide proof points for use in Convincing. Managing positively and effectively the effort in Converting those to new roles where required is extremely important from an organizational motivation perspective. Coaching is a time investment that is definitely required for leading transformations. Make the investment yourself or through others in the organization that can be examples and support your team coaching strategy. The 4 C's (Champion, Convince, Convert or Coach) are strategies for accelerating Change Velocity by understanding the dynamics of willingness and capability for individual team members.

I want to leave you with **three questions** to consider as you create Change Velocity in your organization:

1. What are the Change Views, Change Reactions, and Change Motivations for the individuals, departments, and overall organization?
2. Where are the individuals, departments, and organization in terms of willingness and capability?
3. How and where will you need to Champion, Convince, Coach, and Convert to deal with the questions of what is better and different?

Bottom line: Are you ready to create Change Velocity?

CHAPTER SEVEN:

CREATING BELIEVERS

Getting the team on board! Rallying the troops! The cliché expressions come in many forms. But, the bottom line is that you as the leader must create believers in your vision, the change required and the end goal. Belief in the destination is critical for motivating change. Now, belief is a powerful word. You hear it described as confidence, faith or trust in something or someone. And the believing starts with you.

Change Frame Model

We use the above Change Frame Model in our work. At the center of the change frame are two words – "Why Change?" That question starts with you; you must consider your personal change view, change reaction and change motivation. I have a pragmatic change view myself, so I understand for me the importance of examples, cases and proof or at least the requirement for me to do the math and make sure that the numbers add up, before I can commit to the change. When leading change and with the requirement to create believers, you must know yourself. Where are you in your reaction to the change: denying, resisting, exploring or committing? How motivated are you to lead the change? These are the very same questions you will need to consider for the organization, your team and the individuals across your organization.

CREATING BELIEVERS

A focus on beliefs, attitudes, and creating believers is critical for driving transformational change. During transformational initiatives within an organization, you frequently hear all about the new goals for the organization, followed by a long list of priorities, to do's, work streams and initiatives listed in presentations and assigned to team members. I was just at lunch with a young man yesterday who works in a very large global logistics company. He shared his frustration with all of the analysis and presentations, but lack of action. Now, if the presentations were motivating enough to move the minds and hearts of the audience, just maybe there would be action. But, I have rarely seen a presentation announcing the need to win the hearts of employees, colleagues and associates to make a transformation reality. People are the fulcrum for change, so those people must believe in the need for change. This is particularly true for the customer-facing roles, as these roles will make the transformation a reality for your customers. However, delivering true customer delight is an interdependent achievement—everyone in the organization impacts the customer experience. Maybe this is the reason that transformations are so frequently initiatives rather than realities. As we discussed in Chapter Three, understanding and being clear on the nature, or the core values, of the organization's team members is critical to achieving transformation. And as emphasized in that discussion, the leader of the transformation must also be clear on the organization's core values. How do the core values of the organization and the individuals in the organization align with the desired transformation? Disparity between the desired state, the Z, and the core values of the organization creates friction that slows Change Velocity. The time to move from your A to your Z is impacted by the extent of this disparity.

You remember the example of sweet tea used in Chapter Three to discuss change in appearance, nature and character. As the change moves from action to activity to habit, belief is established and transformation occurs. But when the next transformation is required, we must create believers all over again. The importance of having a core set of values that frame all transformations becomes very important when you look at the next transformation required. You must create believers not only in the cause, the specific transformation, but also in the organization. Believers must be aligned in values first before they travel towards their destination. This is where disparity becomes a factor and there can be lots of friction as you move from your A to your Z. If the change does not align with the core value of the organization or the individuals, get ready for sparks to fly. Unfortunately, the sparks are frequently not visible to the leaders. This is when you lose believers, when the transformations you lead are not aligned with your core values, and those involved begin to doubt your core values. What message are your transformational initiatives sending? How do these messages align with the core values of the organization? How aligned are the organizational values with the values of the individual team members?

SERVANT LEADERSHIP

Extremely important to leading a transformation is testing the formal and informal message of the transformation against the core values of the organization. Now, as all leaders know, the informal message is very powerful within an organization. Remember: you can't not communicate. So, being with the team and having believers that can provide the informal feedback is extremely important to leading a transformation. One of the best at this was a leader for the European operations of a large global technology company that we worked with. This leader was in with the team, living, breathing, working and most importantly leading the transformation. When the country leaders were in for their leadership development programs, this leader participated fully in the sessions. Not a simple kick-off and discussion of how important the session was for the country leaders. He shared experiences, identified roadblocks and developed strategies, actions, activities and organizational habits to drive the transformation. They were committed to the required transformation, but more importantly to the team. Whether you call it the engaged leader, inverted pyramid leader or the servant leader, the focus is on the team, with a true concern for preparing each individual for success.

Personally, I prefer the term **servant leader** for several reasons, and it all goes back to the core values ingrained in me through working on my father's asphalt crew. One of his core values is that you have to shovel with the crew. Putting the asphalt down quickly is important for several reasons, such as better adherence, better compaction and keeping the trucks turning to get the job in more quickly. Some days, the shoveling took longer than anything else. Regardless of your defined role, when there was shoveling to be done, we all knew that he expected us to shovel with the shoveling crew. On the job, it was expected that we take care of each other in whatever ways necessary: bringing your teammate a cup of water on a brutally hot summer day in Georgia, sharing your sandwich because they had none, telling a great story to bring joy in the midst of tiring work. I was never very mechanical, and the crew knew this very well. So, they coached and helped me whenever I needed to repair something onsite. Helping each other was a core value. This may be why as my wife frequently reminds me, I am not very good at asking for help. I never really had to ask. The collective 'we', the asphalt crew, where I learned many of my early work habits was not about asking for help, it was about giving help. Giving was another lesson that I took away from the crew. Belief in working, helping, sharing and giving, not a bad set of core values from summers on the asphalt crew.

So, as you look at your organization—what are your core values? What are your team's core competencies? How aligned is the transformation that you are driving with your team's core values? How do their core competencies align with the requirements of the transformation? Changing core values is a much bigger order than changing competencies. Your core values as a leader will impact how you lead your team, the core values they embrace, and the ways they approach new challenges. The team wants to know that you care about them. As a servant leader, your job is to put the team and the organization before your own self-interest. Are you willing to sacrifice yourself for others? As a leader, this means sometimes taking the big waves for the team and consistently showing them that you are in the boat rowing with them or trying to calm the waters to make the rowing easier for them. They need to hear the story of the Promised Land, the Z. Can you tell a story of the Z that will motivate your team? They want to know that you believe. Do you believe in the final destination enough to row with them? Are you ready to be the leader and calm the raging seas? They want to know that others believe. Are you creating believers who will spread the belief to others and multiply the power of your team? This sounds like a tall order, but not when you believe in the transformation. When you believe, the journey will always be worth the rowing to reach your destination.

If you have a sales transformation in your future, remember Change Velocity is the secret. At the heart of creating Change Velocity is a knowledge of your Change View, Change Reaction and Change Motivation; a willingness to be a servant leader; an ability to create believers in your Z, or your final destination. Speed is required to consistently execute transformation in your organization in an environment of Rapid Dissemination, Faster Creation, and accelerated Time To expectations. My wish is that Change Velocity will take you and your organization farther, faster than you ever expected.

You can assess your organizations transformation readiness at:

http://www.SoarPerformanceGroup.com/Change-Velocity-Diagnostic

I want to leave you with **three questions** to consider as you identify what needs to be transformed in your organization:

1. How well can you tell your transformational story?
2. How ready are you to be a servant leader in the transformation?
3. How ready are you to create believers?

Bottom line question for you: Do you really believe in the transformation?

APPENDIX A: KEYWORDS

INTRO

Transformation: a change in form, appearance, nature or character

Change Velocity: Change View x Change Reaction x Change Motivation

CHAPTER ONE: WHY DOES CHANGE HAPPEN FAST?

Pivot Factor: a thing upon which progress or success depends

Rapid Dissemination: the increased rate at which information travels in the world today, due to greater connectivity and great proximity of that connectivity

Wearables: technology that is worn on the body

Thinkables: devices that respond to our thoughts rather than our physical or verbal commands

Imaginables: products that are created directly through the power of imagination

Gas Pump Phenomenon: the introduction of self-serve pay at the gas pump, the first step in normalizing self-service in the marketplace and shortening the distance between distributor and consumer

Faster Creation: the accelerated pace at which products are created, connections between people are formed, and businesses are grown

Time To: the customer expectation of how long a service should take, increasing demands on producers

CHAPTER TWO: WHAT IS CHANGE VELOCITY?

Velocity: the time rate of change of position of a body in a specified direction

Turning Point: while moving at a fast pace, a racecar driver, or a sales executive, must look ahead to react to a turn before reaching it

CHAPTER THREE: WHAT IS TRANSFORMATION?

Burning Platform: a circumstance that will create an impetus for change in an organization

CHAPTER FOUR: WHAT NEEDS TRANSFORMATION?

First Slice Phenomenon: an unintentional focus on the first slice of the transformation pie, leaving less time and fewer resources to satisfy the requirements of each stage of transformation

Leading Indicator: measures of organizational progress based on activities that result in the future goals of the organization

Lagging Indicator: measures of organizational progress based on past results

Activities: actions executed on a repeatable basis

Actions: things done in response to a specific situation

CHAPTER FIVE: FROM STRATEGY TO EXECUTION

Curious Whys: questions that drive the organization to look deeply at their business interrelationships in order to facilitate the cause and effect thinking required in the Business Model Approach

Business Model Approach: a cause & effect tree that focuses on understanding how a business makes money, the key levers for making money and the key indicators leading to a desired result

Closed Loop: an internal feedback loop from strategy to execution consisting of four elements: action, activity, measurement, and refinement

CHAPTER SIX: CREATING CHANGE VELOCITY

Change View: an individual's normal perspective regarding change. There are three kinds: Status Quo Change View, Pragmatic Change View, and Initiator Change View

Change Reaction: an individual's response to a specific change. There are four phases: denying the need for change, resisting the change, exploring the change, and committing to the change

Change Motivation: the logical and emotional compensation necessary to push an individual or team through a necessary change

CHAPTER SEVEN: CREATING BELIEVERS

Servant Leader: a leader who is willing to sacrifice for his or her team, putting the needs of the organization and team first

APPENDIX B:
CHAPTER SUMMARY QUESTIONS

CHAPTER ONE: WHY DOES CHANGE HAPPEN FAST?

I want to leave you with **three questions** to consider as you look ahead for your next transformational pivot factors:

1. How is "Rapid Dissemination" impacting your customers, their customers and their suppliers?

2. How is "Faster Creation" impacting your customers, their customers and their suppliers?

3. How is "Time To" impacting your customers, their customers and their suppliers?

Bottom line: Is your organization ready to deal with the accelerating rate of change?

CHAPTER TWO: WHAT IS CHANGE VELOCITY?

I want to leave you with **three questions** to consider as you strategically accelerate from where you are to where you want to be:

1. How clear is the organization on its Z- where it wants to be?

2. How clear is the organization on it's A- where it is today?

3. What are the turning points required to get where you want to be?

Bottom line: Is your organization moving quickly enough in driving the desired transformation?

CHAPTER THREE: WHAT IS TRANSFORMATION?

I want to leave you with **three questions** to consider as you look ahead to your next transformation initiative:

1. How well does the leadership team understand the meaning of transformation?

2. How committed is the leadership team to making sweet tea—initiating change in form, appearance, nature, *and* character?

3. How well does where you want to be align with the nature (core beliefs) of your team?

Bottom line: Is your leadership team ready to make transformation happen?

CHAPTER FOUR: WHAT NEEDS TRANSFORMATION?

I want to leave you with **three questions** as you consider what needs to be transformed in your organization:

1. How will you proactively create the right slices for your transformational pie? (Revelation, Determination, Communication, Acceleration, Indication)

2. How will you ensure the right ingredients are in place?

3. How will you avoid the First Slice Phenomenon?

Bottom line: Does your leadership team understand what really needs to be transformed?

CHAPTER FIVE: FROM STRATEGY TO EXECUTION

I want to leave you with **three questions** to consider as you move from strategy to execution:

1. How well does the organization understand the business model and the cause & effect tree?

2. How will you create the closed loop from Action to Activities to Measurement to Refinement?

3. How are you creating a focus on the curious whys in your organization?

Bottom line: Does your organization understand the key levers that will drive the results?

CHAPTER SIX: CREATING CHANGE VELOCITY

I want to leave you with **three questions** to consider as you create Change Velocity in your organization:

1. What are the Change Views, Change Reactions, and Change Motivations for the individuals, departments, and overall organization?

2. Where are the individuals, departments, and organization in terms of willingness and capability?

3. How and where will you need to Champion, Convince, Coach, and Convert to deal with the questions of what is better and different?

Bottom line: Are you ready to create Change Velocity?

CHAPTER SEVEN: CREATING BELIEVERS

I want to leave you with **three questions** to consider as you identify what needs to be transformed in your organization:

1. How well can you tell your transformational story?

2. How ready are you to be a servant leader in the transformation?

3. How ready are you to create believers?

Bottom line: Do you really believe in the transformation?

ABOUT THE AUTHOR

 Charlie Thackston has a passion for helping companies grow. This passion led to the founding of SOAR Performance Group, a consulting and training company, where he serves as president. SOAR Performance Group has a constant focus on helping clients drive changes in go-to-market strategy, sales approach and sales skills to achieve new levels of performance. His prior experience includes sales and marketing leadership roles for early stage venture capital backed technology companies. In these roles, he was responsible for building sales teams, sales channels and product positioning strategies to support successful initial public stock offerings. He holds Master's and Bachelor's Degrees in Business Administration from the Terry College of Business at the University of Georgia.

Charlie lives with his wife, Gayle, in Atlanta. You can reach him at the SOAR Performance Group web site: http://www.SoarPerformanceGroup.com

A FEW FINAL THANK YOU'S

I want to say a very special thank you to Alison Leung for the development of the graphics for this book. She was timely, creative and responsive in creating graphics to help tell the Change Velocity story.

My next thank you is to Chris Hamilton of Chris Hamilton Photography for the author photo production to support the book promotion.

My final thank you is to you, the readers of <u>Change Velocity: The Secret to Leading a Successful Sales Transformation</u>. May you reach your Z!

Made in the USA
Monee, IL
14 August 2024

63935869R00069